IF YOU PROMISE NOT TO TELL

written and
illustrated by
joe wayman

ISBN 0-945799-04-7

ISBN 0-945799-04-7

HEARTSTONE PRESS INC. 1991, Houston, TX
Written and illustrated by Joe Wayman

First published in the United States in 1991
by Heartstone Press Inc.

Dedicated to
Andrea Carlton
and
Ina Tober

In Loving Friendship

CORNERS

May I share a little corner,
Of my life, just one or two?
Perhaps they'll seem familiar,
As if you had lived them too.

If our corners seem a bit alike,
Then just perhaps it's true:
You're a little bit like me,
And I'm a little bit like you.

I HATE TO WAIT

I hate to wait for buses.
I hate to wait for trains.
I hate to wait for streetcars.
I hate to wait for planes.

I hate to wait for growing up.
I hate to wait to cry.
I hate to wait to laugh out loud.
I hate to wait to try.

Now patience is a virtue,
At least that's what they say.
But I never seem to have it,
When I wait for Saturday.

I hurry up and get there,
I'm never, never late.
I hurry, hurry, hurry,
Then I turn around and wait!

And now I'm waiting for a friend,
He said he might be late.
So I wrote this book without him,
'Cause I really hate to wait!

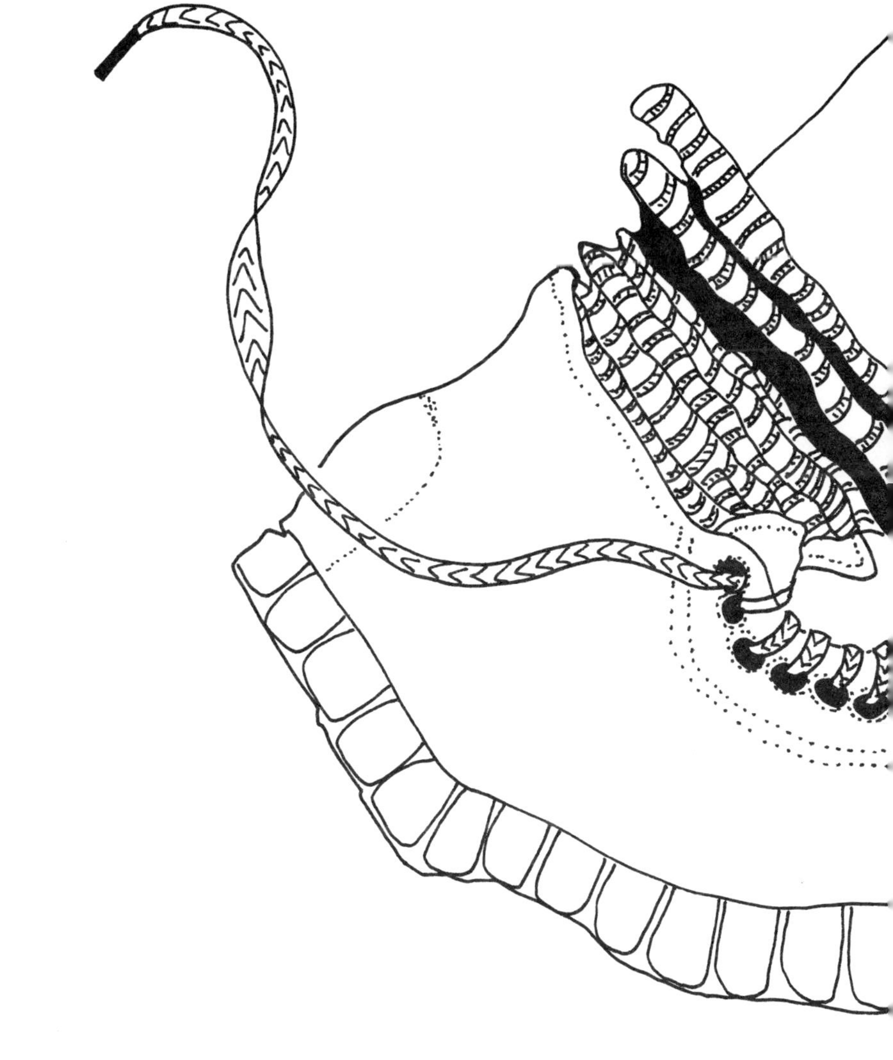

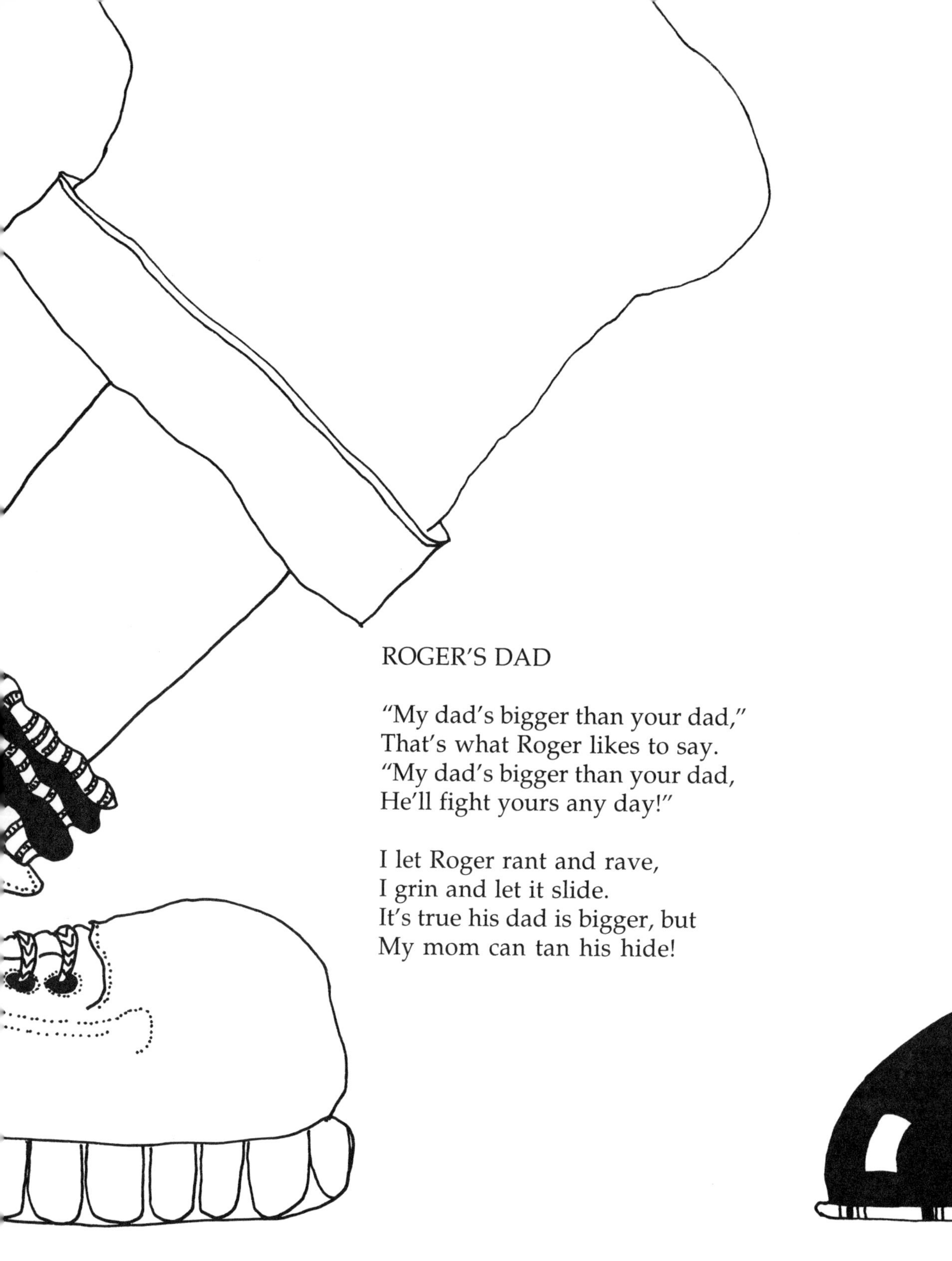

ROGER'S DAD

"My dad's bigger than your dad,"
That's what Roger likes to say.
"My dad's bigger than your dad,
He'll fight yours any day!"

I let Roger rant and rave,
I grin and let it slide.
It's true his dad is bigger, but
My mom can tan his hide!

ALL DRESSED UP

I want to wear my orange shirt,
The one with yellow patches.
"OK," says Mom, "and choose some pants,
But pick a pair that matches."

"All right," I say, and grab the plaid,
The purple and the blue.
I like this pair the very best,
Mom says she likes it too.

Now I need a pair of socks,
These will be just right.
The red ones with a touch of green,
I like them 'cause they're bright.

Now I'm dressed up, all decked out,
Looking good from head to toe,
I dash into the kitchen,
Just as Mom yells, "Time to go!"

Mom looks at me, and smiles,
She's so very proud.
Even though my choices,
Are just a little loud.

She straightens out my collar,
And I hear her gently say,
"You remind me of a rainbow,
On a rainy, rainy day."

BABY SISTER'S BLANKET

I have a little sister,
Who has a blanket and you know,
She drags that silly blanket,
Everywhere she wants to go.

Blanket in her hand,
And sucking on her thumb,
She seems to be in joyful bliss,
It seems a little dumb.

She drags that blanket out of bed,
At the start of every day.
From bed to bath to breakfast,
It drags behind her all the way.

She drags it to the kitchen.
She drags it to her chair.
She drags it out into the yard.
She drags it everywhere.

She clutches it from dawn to dusk,
Won't let it leave her sight.
If you even think of touching it,
You're asking for a fight.

Ridiculous is what I think.
Absurd is what I say.
Deplorable behavior,
Why does she get her way?

That blanket is disgusting,
Simply a disgrace,
Gathering most anything,
Dragging place to place.

They ought to end it here and now,
Lay down the law and let her know!
After all, I gave my blanket up,
At least a year ago!

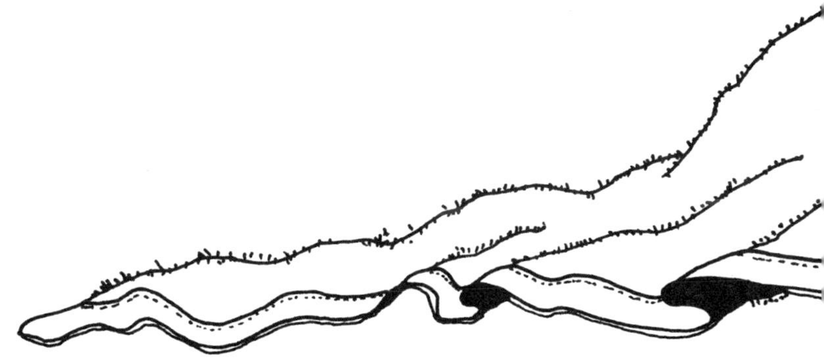

SISTERS, SISTERS

I have two little sisters,
Darlings I am told.
Aunts and uncles all agree,
They're lovely to behold.

Pinafores and ribbons,
Satin, silk and lace.
Curls and locks and patent shoes,
Smiles upon their face.

So well-mannered, well-behaved,
Angels no debate.
They have them all bamboozled,
So I'll set the record straight.

The first one sticks her chewing gum,
Underneath the chair.
She always cheats at jump rope,
And screams it isn't fair!

The second spread the jelly down,
Across her brand-new dress,
Then ran to snitch to Mom and Dad,
How I had made the mess.

They dump the toy box upside down,
Pop balloons for spite.
Scribble on the bathroom wall,
And stay up half the night.

Sisters on the outside,
Are sweet, or so they seem.
Sisters on the inside,
Are really downright mean!

So here's a fact I leave with you,
I'll tell you straight and true,
Brothers never act like that,
But sisters always do!

BROTHER!

MOTHER, DO I HAVE TO?

Mother, do I have to?
How come? It isn't fair!
Every time I turn around,
My little sister's standing there.

Watch your little sister!
Mother says she gets to play.
My friends all groan and roll their eyes,
I'm stuck with her again today!

She's too small to hit the ball.
She can't catch or run.
Then I have to wipe her nose,
She ruins all our fun.

Summer after summer,
She had to go along.
I always had this shadow,
And I called her Tag Along.

Now Tag Along is married,
Has some shadows of her own.
And if I want to play some ball,
I get to go alone.

Yet, somehow I feel sad,
With no Tag Along around.
When the only shadows on the lot,
Are the shadows on the ground.

I love you little shadow,
I knew it even then.
How I'd love to roll the years away,
So you could tag along again.

RICKAFRITZ and RACKAFRATZ!

Rickafritz and rackafratz,
My mother used to say
When she started getting angry,
And didn't get her way.

It's easy when you know it,
You'll learn it right away,
Say rickafritz and rackafratz
To get you through the day.

When you're waiting for the bus,
And it rains upon your head.
When you're eating macaroni,
And it hits the floor instead.

When everything is wrong,
And nothing's going right,
And everyone you talk to,
Is looking for a fight.

When you're doing something special,
And your fingers turn to thumbs.
When nothing seems connected,
And the answers just won't come.

There are words that you can scream,
There are words that you can yell.
Try rickafritz and rackafratz,
And yell them down a well!

Rickafritz and giggle,
Rackafratz and smile.
Rickafritz and rackafratz,
And smile a little while.

RUNNING

"Don't run, don't run,"
Moms and dads will say,
"Don't run, don't run,"
But you have to anyway.

First you get the urge,
It starts out deep inside,
At the top of some big hill,
And it cannot be denied.

Your legs just start to pump,
Your feet begin to fly,
You stretch out like a cheetah,
Soon the world is flying by.

The wind whips through your hair,
Your breath is hot and fast,
Your muscles scream, and dance, and sing,
You're free, you're free at last!

Your brain spins like a top,
Your lungs cry out for air,
A pain rips through your side,
But you don't have time to care!

Then as quickly as it started,
Your body crumples to the ground,
Catch your breath, catch your breath,
Heart pounding, slowing down!

Moms and dads are often right,
But they'd have a lot more fun,
If only every now and then,
They'd go ahead and run!

Button, button, who's got the button?
My belly button's gone, you know.
I have a question just for you,
Where'd my belly button go?

I got up this morning,
Went to wash my face.
Suddenly I noticed
A very empty place.

My belly button was in front,
So I could always know,
When I put my blue jeans on,
Which way they should go.

When you pushed my belly button,
It always made me laugh.
I laughed so hard I almost died,
I laughed so hard I cried.

Without a belly button,
How can I get along?
Now I can't push it when I'm sad,
To turn the laughter on.

And now my button's disappeared,
It simply isn't there.
I'm really sad, I'm so upset,
But no one seems to care.

So everyone please take a look,
Will you check and see,
If you have an extra belly button,
You could lend to me?

KITE

My kite flew, as many do,
not too high and
not too
far.

Tugging
restlessly,
at the end of its
string.

My kite was built of
brittle sticks,
stuck together as no
other.
Impatient on the ground.
Unhappy being bound.
Crying out for
windy weather.

And then one day
it broke its string
and took off on the wind.

It jumped into
the sky,
raced across a field of
yellow daisies,
and, winking and flashing,
flew rambunctiously
away.

Then it took a breath
and dropped,
ssccrruunncchh!
into a pyracantha
bush.

Oh, but for a moment,
such
delicious
wonder!

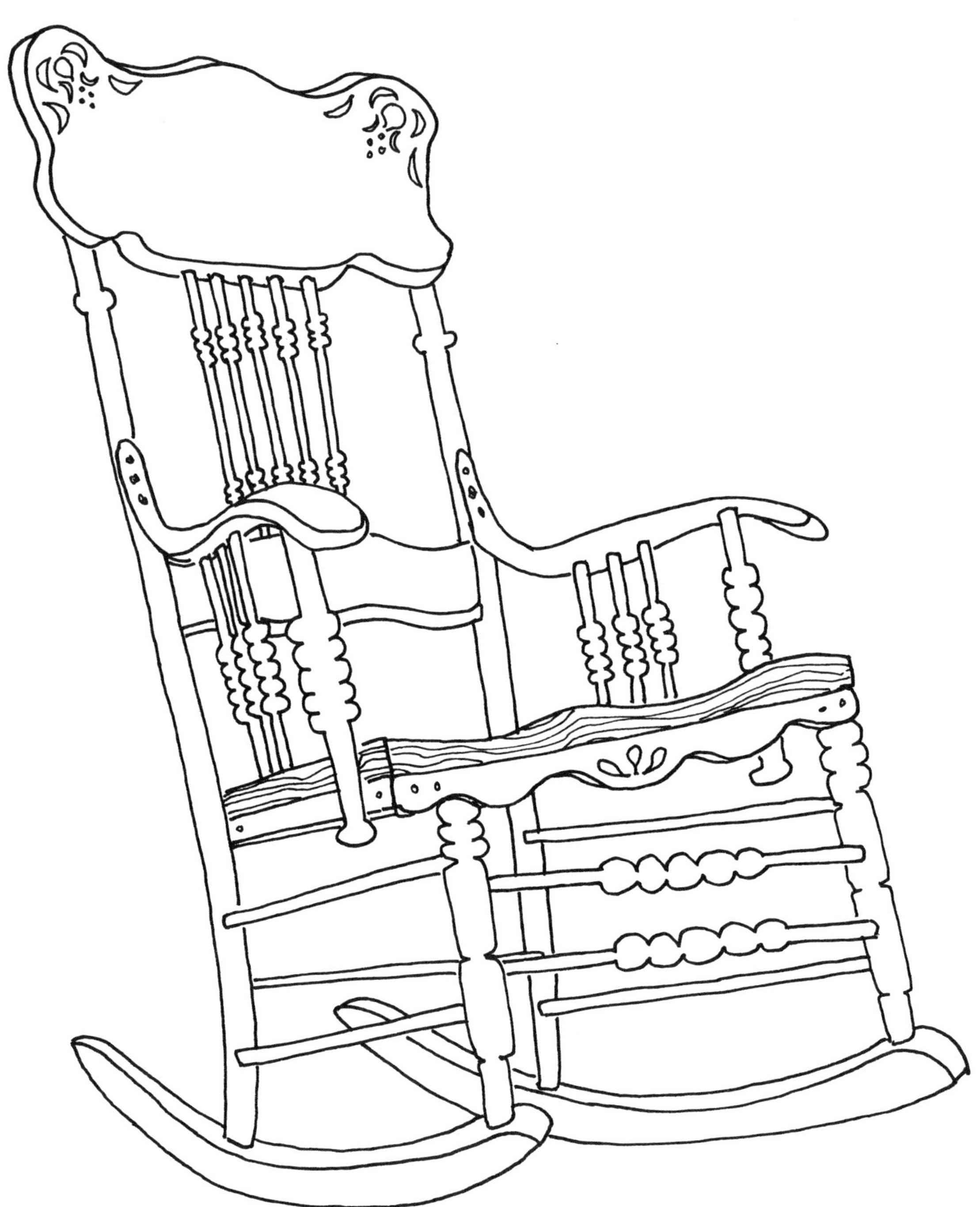

ROCKING CHAIR

Sit up there
on
Grandpa's lap.
Or Uncle Tug's lap.
Or Grandma's lap.
And rock, and
rock and
rock.

squeak. squeak.
squeak. squeak.

Snuggle into soft cotton blouses,
or rough work shirts,
or tough canvas overalls.

squeak. squeak.
squeak. squeak.

Surrounded by
gentle arms and
large, callused,
caring
hands.

squeak. squeak.
squeak. squeak.

And soon you'll be
sound
asleep
and
very, very
safe.

squeak.
squeak.
squeak.
squeak.

WATERMELON SUMMER

Great, pink, half-moons
of frosty,
dripping
watermelon
are handed out
to anxious
summer
hands.

Bending over,
real far,
you bite
one clean, crisp
crescent
from the deep,
sweet center
of that melon.

It runs from both
corners of your mouth,
down your chin,
onto your shirt,
trails across
your jeans and
lands
in rosy circles
on your
summer
tennis shoes.

You spit
hard black seeds
in frantic
arcs
into the
summer park.
And you wonder
if a watermelon
patch
will sprout there
next spring.

You swallow
deeply and feel
more than one
sneaky seed
slide, uninvited,
into your stomach.

You wonder if what your father said
was true:
"Swallow even one,"
he warned,
"and you'll soon
have watermelon vines
growing from your
nose!"

You laugh your
summer laugh and
secretly promise
to never,
ever,
swallow
another slippery
summer
seed.

That summer promise
never
lasts.

WHERE IS A RAINBOW?

I saw a rainbow once,
Drifting in the sky.
My science teacher told me
It was only in my eye.

It made the heavens sparkle,
A simply wondrous sight.
My science teacher said
It was just a trick of light.

He said rainbows were refractions,
Just the bending of the light.
That they didn't speak of hope or joy,
Of good or bad, or wrong or right.

He said life is made of molecules,
Exact and perfectly precise.
And rainbows don't have meaning,
Beyond equations quite concise.

I'd like to meet my science teacher
Once before I'm done.
I'd like to teach him something
I learned when I was young.

You can see a rainbow many ways,
And if you're very smart,
You won't see them with your eyes,
You'll see them with your heart.

FLOWERS

Ick! Ick!
Dirty trick!
They send you flowers
when you're sick.

Wouldn't it be
simply swell
to get those flowers
when you're
well?

A ROSE WAS A ROSE

When I was ten years old,
I gave my mom a rose,
Growing in a plastic pot.
$2.98 was quite a lot.

I dug a hole by our back stair,
And gently planted it right there.
As summer came and quickly passed,
That tiny rose, bloomed full at last.

Then the winter came around,
Snow would soon be on the ground.
Frozen clouds would fill the sky,
And I just knew that rose would die.

So when that first white blanket fell,
That rose was covered deep and well.
I dug it out, I gave it air,
I cleared it off and left it bare.

But little did I know,
As I cleared away that snow,
I'd sentenced death upon that rose,
For late that night it simply froze.

I'd taken its one chance away,
As I stripped it of its quilt that day.
I learned a lesson late that night,
About sometimes holding on too tight.

If life and love will thrive and grow,
Just like roses in the snow,
The lesson that by now you know,
It's best, at times, to just let go.

MY SPECIAL SECRET

I had this special secret,
John said that he could keep it.
He swore he'd never, ever tell,
Then turned around and leaked it!

Yes, my friend John blabbed to Pete,
Pete told his friend Glenda.
She told Janet, Janet ran,
And dribbled it to Brenda.

Brenda went to Brad,
Who spread it all to Phyllis.
Phyllis told it right out loud,
To Lois, Lon and Willis.

Now Willis has this friend,
As true as true can be.
"Promise not to tell," he said,
As he whispered it to me!

ME, MYSELF AND I

40

Some days I throw a party,
And the only guest is me.
I set a very special date,
And plan it carefully.

Then I arrive all by myself,
I'm prompt and right on time.
I ask me how I'm doing,
And I'm always doing fine.

I invite myself to sit right up,
It must be time to dine.
I have a conversation,
With just me, myself and I.

I tell myself I'm glad I came,
And kindly take my place.
I missed myself when I was gone,
It's good to see my face.

I might just stay on through the night,
Party left and party right.
I do enjoy myself you see,
I simply love my company.

Parents, elders, preachers, teachers,
Tell us we are social creatures.
Don't they know that equally,
I need some time alone with me?

BILLY WAYNE ROGER ALPHONSO THE THIRD'S FAVORITE

Mary told me that the one she liked best,
Much better she said, than all of the rest,
Was double-delicious, chocolate-fudge crunch.
She'd eat it from morning till way after lunch.

Johnny told me that the one he liked best,
Much better he said, than all of the rest,
Was triple-whipped marshmallow, cashew delight.
He'd eat it from dinner on into the night.

Linda told me that the one she liked best,
Much better she said, than all of the rest,
Was raspberry-raisin, pistachio-pecan.
She'd eat it from midnight till just after dawn.

And Billy Wayne Roger Alphonso the Third,
Looked at me blankly and said just one word.
And the word that I heard seemed simply absurd,
For the one he liked best was vanilla!

OODLES OF NOODLES

Had to make spaghetti,
Threw it in a pot.
Grabbed a bag of noodles,
You know a little makes a lot.

Stirred it up, boiled it down,
Watched the noodles bubble.
As they boiled, as they cooked,
They doubled and re-doubled.

They grew and swelled and overflowed,
Getting bigger as they cooked.
The package had instructions,
I guess I should have looked.

Those noodles first were ankle deep,
Then they reached up to my knees.
Now I'm in noodles to my nose,
Won't someone help me please!

Soon I fear the house will be,
Submerged in noodles going wild.
The house, the car and Fred the cat,
What have you done my child?

So I fed my baby sister some.
Ate a plate myself.
Froze some for November,
And stuffed some on the shelf.

Sent a roaster full to Grandma,
And a pound to Uncle Jack.
And still I had enough to fill,
Fourteen grocery sacks!

Poodles won't eat noodles,
I should know, I tried.
Goldfish won't eat noodles,
I tried it...they died.

So remember when you fix them,
When you throw them in a pot,
Read DIRECTIONS carefully,
'Cause a little makes a lot!

BORED

I'm bored.

Go ride your bike.
Don't want to ride my bike.

Go play ball.
Don't want to play ball.

Go paint a picture.
Don't want to paint a picture.

Go play with your brother.
Don't want to play with my brother.

Go build a hut out back or jump rope.
Don't want to build a hut or jump rope.

Go clean your room.
See you later,
think I'll go
ride
my
bike.

DOING TIME

Jump rope jingle,
Jump rope rhyme,
I'm gonna sing it,
One more time.

I'm gonna scream,
I'm gonna yell,
If you don't stop that,
I'm gonna tell!

I'll tell Mom,
And I'll tell Dad,
And you'll be sorry,
'Cause they'll be mad.

Don't make me do it,
Don't make me tell,
Don't make me tattle,
Don't make me yell!

I knew you wouldn't listen,
I knew you wouldn't stop!
Instead of telling Dad,
I'm gonna call a cop!

You'll be sorry,
You'll go to jail.
Throw away the key,
You can't pay bail.

Tell it to the jury.
Tell it to the judge.
Makes no difference,
The judge won't budge.

Gavel on the bench,
The judgment's clear.
Twelve long months,
You get one full year!

JanuaryFebruaryMarch
AprilMayJune
JulyAugustSeptember
OctoberNovemberDecember!

Jump rope jingle,
Jump rope rhyme,
I'm gonna sing it,
One more time...

PRETEND

Pretend to be a jump rope
Someone else is jumping.
Pretend to be a big bass drum
Someone else is thumping.

Pretend to be a crocodile
Living in a swamp,
Eating everything in sight,
Chomp! Chomp! Chomp!

Pretend to be a baseball bat
Someone else is swinging.
Pretend to be a silly song
Someone else is singing.

Pretend to be a kangaroo
Ready for a jump,
Heading for a distant hill,
Thump! Thump! Thump!

Be something very simple,
Or pretend to be a star.
Your mind can take you anywhere,
Very near or very far.

Listen to me, listen hard,
Don't let your dreaming end.
I beg you come and play awhile,
Let's pretend, let's pretend.

DOGGY, DOGGY

Here doggy, good doggy,
Come and eat my beans.
Sit underneath the table,
And gobble up my greens.

Here doggy, good doggy,
Don't let Daddy know.
If I don't want to eat it,
You can have it down below.

Here doggy, good doggy,
Be patient while you wait.
Then eat up every single crumb,
Of all the stuff I hate!

IN THE HAMPER

In the shadows in the hall,
Something slithered by.
Slipped into the bathroom,
In the blinking of an eye.

I crept up to the doorway,
And slowly peeked around.
That silent, midnight creature,
Was nowhere to be found.

Had it climbed into the hamper,
Where the dirty clothes should be?
Was it grinning in that hamper,
Waiting just for me?

I stood in fright, so late that night,
Surrounded by my fears.
The only sound in all the world,
The pounding in my ears.

Slowly, oh, so slowly,
I reached out and touched the lid.
I opened it a tiny crack,
I don't know why I did.

I peered into the darkest dark,
And two bright eyes glared back.
That creature in the hamper,
Was ready to attack!

Then that creature wiggled,
Began to purr and softly whine.
What are you doing down in there,
You silly cat of mine?

KITTEN

I found a tiny kitten,
In a gutter almost dead.
So weak, so sad, so sick,
It couldn't lift its head.

I gathered it into my arms,
Its body, soft and gray.
I hugged it close and brought it home,
That cold and rainy day.

My kitten has two tiny ears,
And little paws of pink.
A funny, little pointed nose,
A bit unique, I think.

Her appetite is endless,
She eats everything in sight.
Her teeth are sharp as needles,
And her tail just isn't right.

Instead of soft and furry,
That tail is gray and fat.
Oh! My gosh! A small mistake!
I think my cat's a rat!

CHINA
ARGE
URGENT

THE BOX

I found it on the porch,
Sitting by itself.
A great big box with lots of locks,
Addressed to me, myself.

I think it is a present,
Something special and so fine.
I believe it is a wondrous gift,
And it will all be mine.

Who had brought it, put it there?
Who had sent that box?
Was it sent here just for me?
Should I unlock its locks?

So first I thought, "Of course."
I'll open it and see.
But then I thought, "I just don't know."
What could the contents be?

That box is making noises,
As it sits there all alone.
It wiggles and it jiggles,
I think I hear it moan.

Something might jump out,
And snatch me from my socks!
Something deep inside,
Might leap madly from that box!

Something might come after me,
And grab me up for lunch;
Grasp me in its crimson claws,
And slowly start to munch!

So I simply have to say it,
The truth is plain to see:
I am afraid to open it,
Fright has frozen me.

Well, I get afraid at times,
I'm sure that you do too.
But when I am afraid,
What is it I should do?

Open it? I'd like to.
I really think I should.
But fear restrains my hand,
Now I wouldn't if I could.

That box with locks is sitting there,
Out upon the porch.
It has been there since November,
I'll open it of course.

On second thought I think I'll wait,
Till help is on my side.
Could you drop by and help me,
Find out what is locked inside?

CHINA
ARGE

GHOST BUS

Underneath the lamppost,
In the middle of the night,
A ghost bus makes a silent stop,
A strange and fearful sight.

At the bus stop near your corner,
Something big and green climbs down,
It's looking for your bedroom,
It has searched all over town.

You thought it couldn't find you,
That you were safe and you were sound.
You thought that you could hide,
Where you never could be found.

But now it's almost here,
And it loves the dark of night.
There's only one thing left to do.
Sit up! Turn on the light!

NOT A WITCH, NOT A WITCH

If you listened to the kids,
If you listened to the talk,
Then you would be sure,
A witch lived on our block.

She watched us from her window,
Behind curtains made of lace.
We could see her eyes,
But we seldom saw her face.

Just inside her door,
There was a very narrow stair,
Leading up into the darkness,
Leading up into her lair.

She never came outdoors,
But stayed inside to wait,
Until some luckless orphan,
Crossed her yard a little late.

Then she'd throw a spell,
From behind that wall of lace.
And freeze that child to stone,
With surprise upon his face.

With all her cats to help her,
She'd drag him in the door,
Up that dark, dark stairway,
To that dreadful second floor.

And when we passed her house,
We always ran in fright,
Though deep inside our pounding hearts,
We were laughing with delight.

We never left a valentine,
Or stopped on Halloween,
Or sent a happy birthday wish,
Or ask her how she'd been.

And then by chance, one early spring,
I heard my father say,
That poor, old, lonely woman,
Down the block had passed away.

Now that memory echoes,
"Poor old woman passed away."
Not a witch, not a witch,
But it's too late today.

I cannot leave a valentine,
Or stop on Halloween.
I cannot leave a birthday card,
I cannot do a thing.

What's done is done, and I regret,
I wish I could have known,
How older folks will sometimes live,
Behind their curtains all alone.

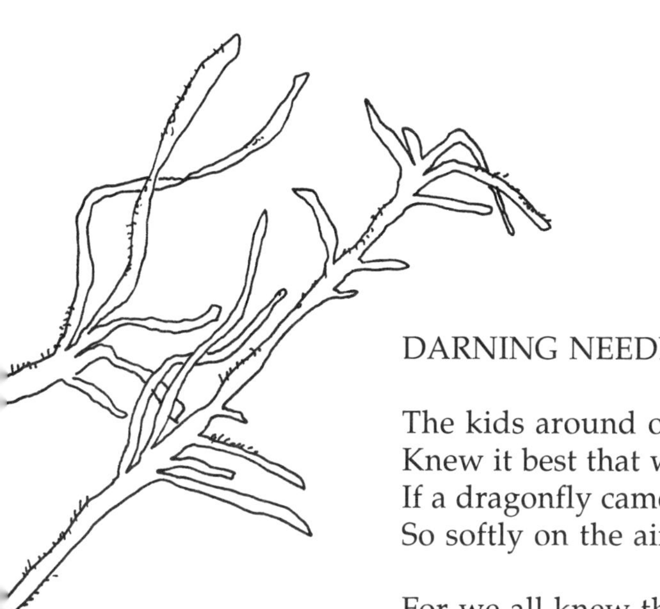

DARNING NEEDLE/DRAGONFLY

The kids around our block,
Knew it best that we take care,
If a dragonfly came flitting by,
So softly on the air.

For we all knew that they
Were darning needles in disguise.
And if you dared to tell a lie,
They'd stitch up both your eyes.

And then they'd sew your lips
Together in a blink,
And zip away across the lawn
Before you had a chance to think.

And so I lived in mortal fear,
Quite sure that if I lied,
I'd soon be stitched from lid to lid,
Until the day I died.

And now I watch the dragonfly,
So fragile and bewitching.
Yes, they're quick as any needles,
But, oh, so innocent of stitching!

SPIN, SPIDER, SPIN

Spin, spider, in the night,
Weave a web of silver light.
Spin, spider, don't take long,
For you must finish with the dawn.

Spin, spider, here's the sun,
Finally your work is done.
Spin, spider, night has fled,
Time for you to go to bed.

Rest, spider, as you do,
I'll dust your web away for you.
Rest, spider, comes the night,
Weave one more web of silver light.

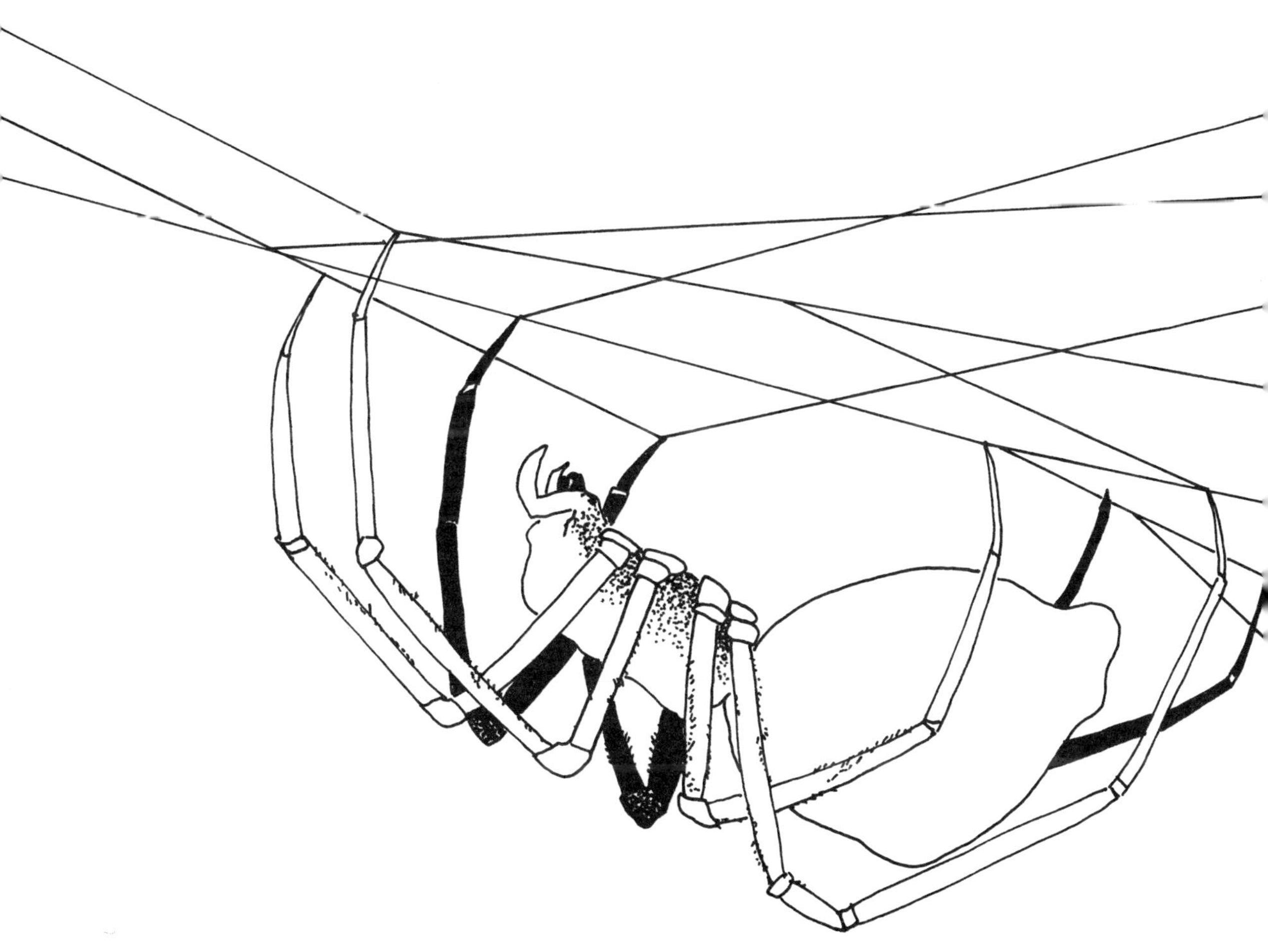

WHEN A GOLDFISH DIES

When a goldfish just decides to die,
There's nothing you can do,
It swims around, upside down,
And suddenly it's through.

Then you'd be surprised,
The way some people act.
They say to flush, they want to rush,
They're mean and that's a fact.

But I wouldn't let them do it,
I said it wasn't fair.
My goldfish spent its life with us,
Doesn't someone care?

"Of course, we care," said Mother,
As she tossed the bowl away!
"Of course, we care," said Father,
As he sent me out to play.

But I couldn't let them do it,
I took my fish along.
I put him in my pocket,
To flush him would be wrong.

I went outside and found a spot,
Laid my goldfish down to rest.
Now I can go to sleep tonight,
I did my very best.

But Mom and Dad will lie awake,
Toss and turn for hours.
They'll have it on their conscience,
They didn't send me flowers.

And now I have a turtle,
Mom said she'll take his place.
But I reserved a little spot,
Beside my goldfish just in case!

FRED
FREIDA

MOONLIGHT NIGHT

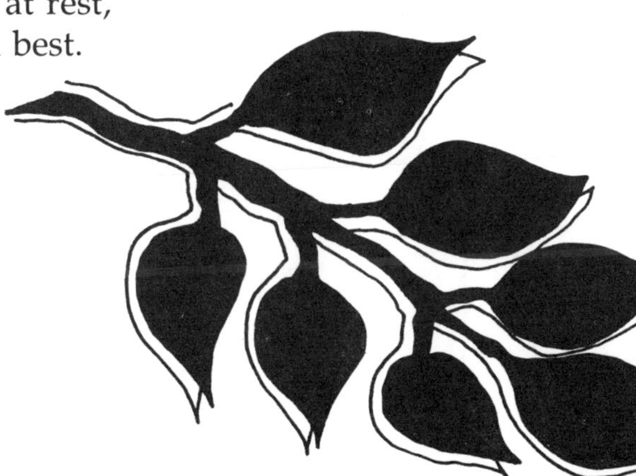

Pale shadows on the ground,
Pale and bereft of sound,
Pale in the darkest night,
Pale in the soft moonlight.

Pale shadow, leaves of black,
Pale branches staring back,
Pale gray the ghostly land,
Pale silver on the sand.

Pale shadow, ashen shades,
Pale fields, your color fades,
Pale moon, the earth at rest,
Pale night, I love you best.

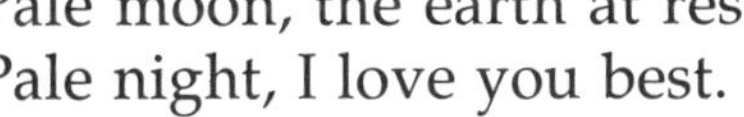

THE GRASS SAID, "NO!"

The grass said,
"No! I will not grow."
The trees said,
"No! We just won't grow."
The flowers said,
"No! We just won't grow."

And the people looked around
Dumbfounded!

The wind said,
"No! I've decided not to blow."
The rivers said,
"No! We just won't flow."
The clouds said,
"No! We won't rain or snow."

And the people looked around
Dumbfounded!

The rain said,
"No! I will not fall."
The whippoorwill said,
"I will no longer call."
The fish said,
"No! We won't swim at all."

And the people looked around
Dumbfounded!

"You chop us all down,
Tramp us to the ground.
Fill us up with trash,
Clutter, smoke and ash.
Choke off our song,
Use us till we're gone."

And the people looked around
Dumbfounded!

And if you are so blind,
That you just cannot see,
Then the world will stop.
It just can't be.
Time will halt,
And it's all your fault.

And the people looked around
Dumbfounded!

Flutterby.
Flutterby.
I love to watch you
flutter
by.

Brushing softly
here and there,
you skim across the
garden
air.

The path you take is
up-and-down,
back-and-forth
above the
ground.

Such a fragile
thing you are,
what need have you
to fly so far?

The wings you beat
so silently
seem painted
in my
fantasy.

Flutterby.
Flutterby.
I love to
watch you
flutter
by.

Butterfly.
Butterfly.
You no longer
flutter
by.

You're dead and
dry
upon a pin.
Tiny violence.
Monumental
sin.

Mounted under
savage glass.
How did this murder
come to
pass?

The magic of your
flight is gone.
They stole away
your joyful
song.

Left you cold and
still in death,
your beauty died with
your last breath.

Butterfly.
Butterfly.
You no longer
flutter
by.

QUESTIONS WITHOUT ANSWERS

What good is joy without the laughter?
Tears without the sorrow?
Pain without the hurting?
Time without tomorrow?

A maker of the peace,
Who has to fight to get his way?
A fighter for the freedom,
Afraid of being free?

What good's a room without a window?
A window without glass?
A song without the singing?
A man without a past?

A dancer without feet?
A runner without races?
A race without an ending,
Through a crowd that has no faces?

What good is rhyme without the reason?
Time without the season?
Age without the beauty?
Youth without the wisdom?

A suitcase standing empty,
Destination still unknown?
A journey that you travel,
If you never travel home?

What good are questions without answers?
Answers without questions?
Like my thoughts without the answers,
The questions are all mine.

INDEX

ALL DRESSED UP...8
A ROSE WAS A ROSE.. 36
BABY SISTER'S BLANKET...10
BELLY BUTTON BLUES.. 22
BILLY WAYNE ROGER ALPHONSO THE THIRD'S..................44
BORED..49
CORNERS...3
DARNING NEEDLE/DRAGONFLY..................................... 73
DOGGY, DOGGY... 57
DOING TIME... 50
FLOWERS...34
FLUTTER BY/BUTTERFLY..86
GHOST BUS.. 66
I HATE TO WAIT..4
IN THE HAMPER..58
KITE.. 24
KITTEN..60
ME, MYSELF AND I..40

HEARTSTONE PRESS INC.
P.O. Box 890686
Houston, TX 77289-0686

ISBN 0-945799-04-7

MOONLIGHT NIGHT...81
MOTHER, DO I HAVE TO?...17
MY SPECIAL SECRET...39
NOT A WITCH, NOT A WITCH...69
OODLES OF NOODLES...46
PRETEND..54
QUESTIONS WITHOUT ANSWERS....................................88
RICKAFRITZ AND RACKAFRATZ.......................................18
ROCKING CHAIR...27
ROGER'S DAD..6
RUNNING...20
SISTERS, SISTERS...12
SPIN, SPIDER, SPIN...74
THE BOX...63
THE GRASS SAID, "NO!"...82
WATERMELON SUMMER..28
WHEN A GOLDFISH DIES...76
WHERE IS A RAINBOW?...33

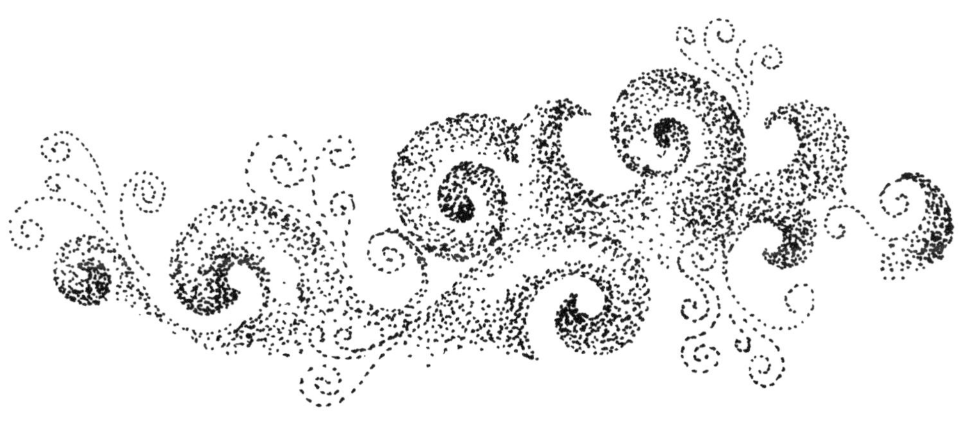

Joe
Wayman!